Understanding the Interregnum

Interregnum

Making Judgments When Kings Move

Tony Bradley

Lay Training Adviser, Diocese of Coventry
Associate Minister, Holy Trinity, Coventry

GROVE BOOKS LIMITED
RIDLEY HALL RD CAMBRIDGE CB3 9HU

Contents

The Cover Illustration is by Hannah Jamieson

First Impression September 1996
ISSN 0144-171X
ISBN 1 85174 325 1

1
Through the Looking Glass

When the vicar announces that he or she is at last moving on the church calls an interregnum. It is as if the king is about to depart. Of course, the truth is that the King never leaves. The so-called interregnum is an unfortunate misnomer.

Even so, the time between one incumbent departing and another being instituted holds enormous potential for a local church. It can be a time for rejoicing in the past works of God, examining the present condition of the church and considering the future to which God is calling his people. An interregnum is—in contemporary parlance—a window of opportunity, through which can be glimpsed a kingdom already prepared, beyond the tiny realm in which vicar's are persuaded to rule, where the Lord is inviting his church to dwell.

This window is a moment for the kingdom of God to be seen more clearly than at other times—not that this is the way most churches look at their interregnum. Instead of being glass stained with the blood of Christ, showing the way of true service, or a mirror, revealing the dim reflection of Jesus Christ in his people (1 Cor 13.12), this window is most frequently boarded-up.

During my few years in Anglican orders I have managed to assist in handling several interregnums.[1] But it was the first such experience, when I was a curate, that taught me most about how this window is viewed. The day after the previous vicar left I was told lovingly, but firmly, by both the parish administrator and one of the churchwardens that nothing must change during the interregnum. I was to assist in effectively moth-balling the church until the new vicar arrived!

Of course, that did not prove possible. The vicar had done such a wonderful job in pastorally caring for his parish and people that many were deeply bereaved at his passing from sight. Consequently, over the next few months I had the task of being bereavement counsellor to more than 100 people inside the church and scores outside, for whom he had been—unintentionally—the visible presence of God. It was, as you might imagine, a challenging period for a young curate.

But, equally, helping people work through bereavement is often about enabling them to manage personal change. As such, many new experiences presented themselves to the people of Christchurch, Southchurch, during that interregnum, which helped them—as well as their previous vicar—to move on into a new place.

---

1 The first was as Assistant Curate at Christchurch, Southchurch, Southend-on-Sea, when Bob Payne moved on to St Matthias, Plymouth,then, subsequently to become Warden of Lee Abbey, Devon. The second was as Associate Minister at Holy Trinity, Coventry, when Graham Dow moved on to become Bishop of Willesden. Since then, as Lay Training Adviser in Coventry diocese I have had the privilege of helping various parishes in our diocese—most notably in the Warwickshire village of Wootton Wawen—to creatively use the interregnum as a time for peering into this looking glass.

Alternative Visions

Nevertheless, the view is widely held that an interregnum is a time for battening down the hatches and surviving, as best we can, the storms of being vicarless.

A few days ago I was part of a meeting to discuss training for collaborative ministry in the country parishes of our diocese, at which two of the rural deans were present.[2] The conversation moved on to how the interregnum experience could be used as a moment for enabling parishes to retrain for future patterns of ministry. Suddenly, the air became electric. It was quite clear that very different standpoints were held on whether or not the interregnum was an appropriate moment for considering change. One rural dean saw the interregnum window as a clear opportunity for looking forwards and out. More negatively, the other argued that it was vital to resist any temptation to introduce new ideas or ministry practices when there was no incumbent around.

His argument was that novelty could lead to a period of retrenchment and losing ground. Moreover, our diocesan guidelines on the handling of interregnums—in line with those in the Church of England's Canons and Standing Orders—were cited in defence of this position. The possibility that decline might arise from resisting new patterns did not seem to be worth considering!

What lay behind these alternative visions? Of course, many influences will bear on why people react in different ways. But I suspect that the main factor affecting the way a local church looks through the interregnum glass is its model of ordained ministry. Where the vicar is seen as the local king (whose institution is a sort of coronation) then it is difficult to avoid the feeling that the interregnum represents a time of uneasy succession. By contrast, in situations where the incumbent is regarded more as a team leader, the window provides an opportunity for assessing what sort of team we are and what sort of leader we need next.

These two alternative models of incumbency represent the technical distinction often drawn between 'ontological' and 'functional' models of ministry,[3] and these were very much to the fore in our diocesan discussion. According to the first model, with ordination—and, especially, incumbency—comes a change in nature, together with a sort of 'divine right.' But according to the 'functional' view, ordination (and institution) is mainly about authorizing a person (parson) to fulfil a particular leadership task, which may be exercised in many different ways or styles.

But does it matter very much which model of incumbency is held? Well, I

---

2   In our context 'collaborative ministry' means the development of local ministry arrangements where lay people share—alongside the clergy—in the formally recognized exercise of Christian service, as part of a team.

3   The basic distinction between 'ontological' and 'functional' models used here is far less sophisticated than that outlined by Ian Bunting, *Models of Ministry* (Grove Pastoral Series No 54, Nottingham: Grove Books, 1993). This dichotomy relates to the extreme destinations reached by going to either end of a spectrum of ministerial models. Each of Bunting's models may be developed from either of these broad destinations, although the Overseer, Competent Professional and Practical Theologian models appear closer to the 'ontological' end. The Minister-in-Community and Community Builder models come closest to the 'functional' end. The Consultant and Middle Manager models adopt a position somewhere in the centre-ground.

want to suggest that it is of great importance how the vicar's status is translated into an understanding of his or her role, because, if the 'ontological' position is dominant, it is curtains for the interregnum as a window of opportunity. The 'vicar has a different nature' view effectively draws a veil across the local church's ministry when there is no vicar in residence.

This vision of ministry disregards the lay styles of leadership and service—collaborating with clergy from elsewhere—that occur in an interregnum. According to the 'ontological' view, those are of little real significance for the continuing exercise of ministry in the church of God. As such, no new light on developing patterns of ministry can come into the parish from outside, at the one time when it is possible to see ministry operating in different ways. Furthermore, I would argue that as the 'ontological' position has dominated within the Church of England, many of the clearest New Testament perspectives on ministry have been contradicted.[4] This restricts the interregnum process to one of surviving a brief period of ruler-less chaos, before normal monarchical service is resumed. Instead of this, I want to suggest that there is a clear biblical mandate for developing a radically alternative vision of what the interregnum can be.

From Judges to Kings

This mandate is most obviously expressed in the period of transition from the time of the Judges to the first kings of Israel and Judah, recorded in 1 Samuel 8 following.[5] Through this narrative we are presented with the ending of the judges, the appointment of Israel's first king, Saul, and his rejection by the Lord.

A cursory reading of the text might suggest that this was the natural next step in Israel's development, as the people of God. As they became more settled—through military victories—in the land beyond the Jordan, it was necessary for them to institute a more dynastic form of rulership. The peripatetic pattern of judgment and decision-making that had marked Samuel's leadership and that of the earlier judges needed to give way to the rule of a monarch (1 Sam 7.15-17).

But if we look closer we see that setting-out on a period of kingship was far from an ideal that God had arranged for his people to walk in. The move towards appointing kings was an idea that came from the people themselves, borrowed from the surrounding nations (1 Sam 8.5–6, 19–20; 12.12–13; 2 Sam 5.1–2). Crucially, it was a sign that Israel had moved from dependence upon divine inspiration to needing a more visible ruler in their midst.

It is for that reason Samuel desperately asks the Lord to deny the popular mood, warning the people what having a king will mean (8.6, 10–18). The king will be able to conscript the young men in times of war. He will commandeer

---

4   There exists a wide range of alternative understandings of ministry, from the so-called 'functional' to the more 'ontological' views. Each of the 'functional' positions can readily be supported from the New Testament. But I am hard-pressed to back up any of the 'ontological' positions from Scripture.
5   It would be worth your reading 1 Sam 8-15 at this point, before proceeding with the next section.

some for the army, some for the 'factories' and some for the fields. The king will also have the right to put the young women to work, to dispose of the best land amongst his generals, to demand taxes in kind and generally to enslave the people. Kings do not look like entirely good news!

Yet, despite the high regard in which Samuel was held, as a genuinely Spirit-led prophet and judge, the people continue to cry out for a king to rule them. So, Samuel prayerfully consults the Lord about this matter (8.21f). Such was his direct relationship with God that the word of the Lord comes clearly to him: 'Listen to them and give them a king.'

The outcome of this is that Saul is anointed, then appointed and, finally, confirmed as king (10.1; 10.24; 11.15). It is not exactly a crisp and straightforward coronation, since all the way through the narrative there is an underlying message: the reason for the people's need of a king is their failure to hear God's word and their rejection of his divine leadership. Ever since the days of disobedience in the desert, after the Exodus from Egypt, the people have been turning away from divine rule (8.7f; 10.17f; 12.6f).

So the conclusion of this narrative sequence comes as little surprise. Saul, once he has been made king, equivocates, turns against his close supporters, including his own son Jonathan, is rejected by the Lord and sees the Spirit depart from him (13.7f; 14.24f; 15.10f; 16.14). A new king has to be found, anointed by the prophet and eventually made king.

The plain message of this major period of Old Testament history is that kings are a decidedly mixed blessing. In the later narratives the rule of the kings is checked by the oracles of the prophets, but in this earlier sequence in 1 Samuel, it appears that the transition in leadership from judges to kings reflects a loss of faith by the people of Israel. It is far easier to rely on a tangible ruler than on the power of prayer to the living God. And a relatively settled, institutionalized monarchy has little need for listening to God's Spirit.

A Time for Right Judgment

All this points to a biblical reason for adopting a more radical approach to handling the interregnum. On the basis of this story in 1 Samuel we might well conclude that appointing a monarchical figure would be a backward step.

In particular, the story of how Israel moved towards adopting rule by kings suggests that the interregnum could involve a reinstatement of the period of 'judges.' Instead of it being an empty gap between the reign of 'ontologically' secure monarchs, it has the potential to be a key time for listening to the Spirit and using sound judgment, before rushing to find a new 'functional' incumbent.

During the interregnum the parish can be helped to judge where it has come from, where it is now and where it is going. These explorations should be useful signposts to the main work of judgment, which is to directly rest on the word of God, through his Spirit. If a parish can do that in interregnum it will be far less prone to being subject to the whims and weaknesses of individual vicar-kings.

2

Putting Kings Into Context

Bridging the Gap

Church-speak about 'interregnums' is misleading. It is unrealistic to imagine that every gap left by a vicar moving looks and feels the same. We would hardly say that each of the transitions between British monarchs—in this century—had been identical. The 'abdication crisis' interregnum was hardly the same as that caused by the death of George VI and which led to the coronation of Queen Elizabeth II. Each and every interregnum is distinct unto itself.

This is partly because the leadership culture of each period of ministry is distinctive, but it is also because interregnums are prompted by very different sets of circumstances. Putting these two factors together, we begin to see that saying 'we are moving into an interregnum' is saying very little in itself—less, indeed, than if we were changing monarchs. The vicar probably has an even less-defined job specification and constitution to work with than a monarch.[6] Consequently, in order to understand how to bridge the gap more effectively, it may be helpful to look at the factors of leadership transition and the circumstances surrounding why interregnums happen.

Take Us to Our Next Leader!

There are many different and varied styles of leadership in all areas of human activity, and the church is no exception. A classic analysis of models of leadership that is helpful in assessing the styles of vicars and church leaders is provided by Tannenbaum and Schmidt.[7] They identify seven gradations of leadership style, along the gradient from authoritarian, through democratic, to *laissez-faire*.

At the most authoritarian end of the continuum all decision-making is leader-centred. In this style of leadership, the vicar simply announces all decisions. By contrast, at the most *laissez-faire* end of the spectrum the group takes as much freedom as it wants to define and decide on issues. Making decisions is team-centred, based on the freedom of group members. Between these two extremes are various positions of democratic accommodation between the leader and the group, involving consultation and joint decision-making.

The fact that vicars can exhibit characteristics of leadership from any point along this continuum will not be news. But is leadership style explicitly taken

---

6   Ian Bunting, *Models of Ministry* (Grove Pastoral Series No 54, Nottingham: Grove Books, 1993) identifies seven alternative models for the core of a vicar's ministry: consultant, overseer, competent professional, practical theologian, minister-in-community, community builder and middle manager models. Which of each of these models a local church has had and needs next will be an additional factor to add to the interregnum algorithm, as we shall describe more fully in the biblical analysis below.

7   Peter Tannenbaum and Warren Schmidt, *Harvard Business Review* Vol 36, No 2 (March 1958), quoted by Peter Wagner, *Leading Your Church to Growth* (London: MARC Europe, 1985) p 100.

into account when a church is looking to appoint its next incumbent, whether by the bishop, patron, parish representatives, PCC or congregation?[8] Problems of mismatch (for vicars as well as churches) could be avoided if questions about appropriate styles of leadership became prominent during the interregnum.

This question of leadership style is particularly important for churches to address in an age when, as John Habgood has recently said, 'there is a deep contempt for authority purveyed by much of the media.'[9] And when people are confused about what authority is appropriate for ministers to exercise, it would be a foolish laity that ignored the question of future leadership style.

As someone asked me recently, 'Which way up is the flowerpot meant to be?' Is authority in the church meant to look like a top-down pyramid, where those in groups, at the base, are instructed by a leader standing on 'his' apex? Or is it meant to be more like a flowerpot, as John Finney describes gospel-centred patterns of leadership in the church?[10] In the flowerpot church, those in the church's groups, who form the widest part of the pot, are enabled to be 'on top' of a narrow base of supportive church leaders.

I firmly believe pyramidal church structures stifle life, whilst flowerpots release it. The pyramids were constructed to contain the dead. By contrast flowerpots are designed to nurture the growing. This is not to say that all churches with 'flowerpot' authority structures can be guaranteed to produce new life. But, they do, perhaps, have more potential for producing vibrant new plants, that are growing in an outward direction, than does the hierarchically ordered church, controlled by a monarchical vicar. This emphasizes the critical nature of placing style of leadership within differing authority cultures onto the interregnum agenda and of using the interregnum to try out alternative styles to the pyramid if authoritarian leadership has been a previous problem.

Mind the Gap!

Just as the leadership styles of clergy are many and various (always recognizing that not all clergy see themselves as gifted leaders) so are the factors occasioning each 'king's' move. The influences prompting an interregnum to happen do quite dramatically affect the way in which a local church 'minds the gap.'

In my own ministry—as curate, associate minister and diocesan officer—I have been partly responsible for covering interregnums and handling departments for bosses after their 'heads' have departed. In each case the feel of the interregnum has been very different, according to the reason for the previous king's move.

My first experience was when, as curate, my vicar moved to a new parish on the other side of the country. Because he went from a vicar's post to becoming a

---

8   The authors of the excellent parallel Grove booklet to this one, by David Field and David Parrott, *Situation Vacant—A Guide to the Appointment Process in the Church of England* (Grove Pastoral Series No 65) should be consulted for details of who is involved and how, in the process of appointing a new vicar, during the interregnum.
9   John Habgood, 'Culture of contempt' in *Leading Light—Christian Faith and Contemporary Culture*, Vol 3, No 1, 1996, pp 5-8.
10 John Finney, *Understanding Leadership* (Daybreak, 1989) pp 27ff.

priest-in-charge the congregation had some (quite erroneous) feelings of being put aside. This meant that a major feature of that interregnum was 'post-loss counselling.'

By contrast, my second interregnum experience came about when our vicar was made a bishop. In this case, although there was still a great sense of loss, the church was able to view the interregnum far more positively from the outset. They were proud of their vicar becoming a bishop and so were able to look to the future with more confidence. This also reflected the fact that this parish had a much more strongly developed pattern of lay leadership and discipleship. In retrospect, however, it took far longer for them to adjust to a new style of leadership than it did in the first, smaller and less confident church. This simply reflects the fact that the 'turning circle' is wider for larger, more developed churches. Smaller churches can often adapt faster to changes of leadership.

My third interregnum experience was quite different again, being within a diocesan department rather than a local parish. The reason for my boss leaving his post as head of department was that he and the diocese wanted him to return to parish ministry, as the rector of a large, prestigious but managerially-challenged team. As circumstances prevailed, there were almost simultaneous changes to several other key diocesan personnel, which effectively caused the department to disintegrate and reconstitute itself, in a different form, over quite a short period. This raised the issue of how churches manage when an interregnum leads to a wholesale redefinition of ministry patterns.

Such redefinition is not so unusual, as interregnums are increasingly being caused by 'pastoral reorganizations' in which parishes are amalgamated and regrouped into multiple benefices and clergy posts are 'rationalized.' In such situations, entirely new teams are created in order to respond to both new mission initiatives and the cold climate for ministry that the church is currently experiencing. But because of the past dependence on a model of the solo vicar as monarch, many parishes are entirely unprepared to face this new situation.

These external changes to the context for local ministry make the case for instituting special times of judgment—when no monarchical vicar is around—most forcibly. We need to look through the interregnum window with a degree of objectivity about the past and present, together with faith for God's future.

The above situations that I have described do not cover anything like the possible circumstances that can prompt interregnums. Here are just a few of the other scenarios that lead to vacancies, together with a few questions that they raise:

- *Retirement*—The vicar leaves the parish at the close of his/her full-time ministry. Everyone wonders how far away s/he's going to live.
- *Death in post*—Whether the death is sudden and unexpected or at the end of a long illness it is always a deep shock. Will people feel able to be honest and truthful about the spiritual legacy s/he leaves behind?
- *Scandal*—It is a sad fact that vicar-kings and queens are not without weakness. How quickly will the church and community recover their trust and faith in

the leadership of the clergy?

- *Resigning orders*—Not all clergy who leave active, ordained ministry do so because of scandal. Some have tragically lost their faith, while others simply see their call as shifting back to a less formal status. What does this say to people about the nature of orders of ministry?
- *New ministries*—By far the majority of interregnums happen as a result of the call to a new parochial ministry. But some are because the vicar feels called to a sector or other specialized ministry, in a different ordained capacity.

These headlines—together with the previous stories—do not exhaust the range of possible factors causing an interregnum. What they do is to further highlight the variety of contexts for this special gap and the potential it offers for looking at new patterns of leadership ministry in the church.

Putting these contexts alongside the continuum of leadership styles outlined above, together with the models of ministry that Ian Bunting identifies, shows something of the possible factor mix that confronts a local church when it is challenged by a king's move. Having to face such complexity should also help us to question the patterns of ministry we have inherited as we look to the emergent church.

In commenting on the typology of Tannenbaum and Schmidt, as interpreted by Peter Wagner, David Cormack suggests that there is considerable scope for us to look at fresh understandings of leadership. He quotes some experiences from wartime to make his point:

'The hypothesis that the behaviour of leaders in one setting may be different from their behaviour in others [has much to commend it]. This was recognized by bomber crews during World War II. They were allowed to 'mutiny' in emergencies, following a crash behind enemy lines…the crew could select a differing commanding officer whose leadership skills better met the new situation.'[11]

Similarly, the interregnum can provide the ideal moment for a church to consider its potential future leadership, in its changing context. But how can a church decide on what sort of leader is right for the next phase of its life? In the following chapter we will look at what the Bible reveals about moving across the leadership gap.

---

11 David Cormack, *Team Spirit—people working with people* (MARC Europe, Eastbourne, 2nd edition, 1990) p 32.

3
One Bible, Many Mandates

In the first chapter we saw how texts from 1 Samuel raised questions about the significance of having judges around. But is there anything that can help us assess how to move from one period of leadership to another? The answer is that there is an enormous amount. The Scriptures are full of examples of leadership transitions and the ways in which alternative 'interregnums' bridge the gaps between God's appointed leaders.

We will look at seven of these narratives in some detail, commenting on the styles of leadership, models of ministry, situations prompting these change-overs, and what they tell us about appropriate moves from one leadership to another. Constraints of space only permit some very thumbnail sketches and the briefest of reflections on these important biblical passages.

Not Quite the Promised Land—Moses to Joshua (Exodus 24; Numbers 27; Joshua)

Moses' name means 'drawn out,' in the sense of being cajoled into ministry by the Lord. As with many vicars, Moses took a considerable time to develop and receive his core vision for leading the people during his ministry. Even so, he became the strongest and most directive leader that Israel had seen.

What distinguishes him above all is that he was called to take people towards the Promised Land. And yet, largely because of the failings of the people during their long wilderness years, Moses was denied access. He could see the land from a distance, but he himself never stood on the far side of the River Jordan. It was left to the ministry of Moses' servant Joshua (Yeshua or Jesus, meaning 'the Lord saves') to win through to the place of promised vision. The clearest point about this leadership transition is that it enabled the promised vision to be achieved, while the key to Joshua's ministry is that he had been Moses' servant for many years. He had heard the vision, been trained in leadership that was directed towards it and, in the later years, been part of those who had shaped it.

The message is that not all vicars who are leading God's people into a clearly defined 'promised land' make it. However, if the people are to get there the successor must be hand-picked by his/her former boss, or by someone close enough to them to have shared the vision from the outset. If this does not happen, the previous journey—led by the great visionary—becomes wasted, like water running into the rocks of the wilderness.

Although it is unusual in Anglican practice for assistant clergy to be offered to take over as vicar, after the 'patriarch's' departure, such transitions are not unknown. Indeed, certain churches have become well-known for passing on the mantle of leadership from senior to junior colleague quite regularly. But these tend to be churches which have an exceptionally clear vision of the direction in which God is leading them.

A 'Moses' vicar must be succeeded by a local Joshua curate, who understands what the previous vicar was trying to do and, more importantly, sees beyond the vicar's vision to the authenticity of God's call. Such an interregnum decision would not be easy. There would be enormous pressure from many of the grumblers to go for a completely new broom. But they would be wrong; only a Joshua can follow a Moses!

An Unlikely Candidate—Saul to David (1 Sam 16; 2 Sam 2)

Saul's reign had begun well despite the many reservations that Samuel had. Although the prophet desperately disapproved of Israel appointing a human king, Saul's authority was fully accepted at first, when he brought the tribes together to fight. The problem was that once established as a warrior-king, who shared the judges' ecstatic prophetic gifts, Saul's power went to his head. He displayed a classic case of leadership paranoia, especially towards David. As often, the other side of the coin of shared ministry is mistrust and competition.

What makes the biblical account of this leadership transition all the more remarkable, however, is the way in which Saul's successor was chosen. David's 'selection conference' was unlike anything CACTM, ACCM or ABM have yet dreamt up. He was not even on the candidates' list when Samuel (as chairman of selectors) came by. Nor did Jesse (his erstwhile DDO) consider David to be suitable—too young, too sexy and too useful, pastorally, to Jesse.

When a ministry has gone as sour as Saul's did—from charismatic leadership to the despotism of desperation—it is obviously time for a change. The parish needs to be open to the possibility of that change being in a quite radical and unforeseen direction.

The people of Israel were willing to take the risky step of trying out a young, radical and almost entirely untested leader, whose bravery captured their imagination. How many parishes miss out on a David because they feel unable to break the repeating cycle of appointing one Saul after another—things always starting well but then going downhill after the first charismatic flourish?

In the Corridors of Power—David to Solomon (2 Sam 13-18; 1 Kings 1-2)

As with many of history's most powerful and successful rulers, David left a power vacuum behind him which was filled—in what are usually called the 'succession narratives'—by a series of young pretenders seeking high office. The leadership transition following David was marked by a most unholy political scrap.

The difficulty was caused by the fact that David had a number of sons by different wives. Of course, David's most significant liaison was the adulterous affair with Bathsheba. It was therefore surprising that Solomon—the child of this relationship—was most beloved by God (12.24). Although God's will triumphed in the end, it was worked out through a most Machiavellian series of manoeuvrings, more akin to the plot of Shakespeare's *Richard the Third*.

Amnon was murdered by Absalom because he had raped his sister; Absalom was killed as a rebel. Adonijar, the next in line, then mounted a further attempted coup, ably supported by the army commander and one of the two chief priests. But they were outflanked by Nathan the prophet and Zadok, the other chief priest, who succeeded in anointing Solomon king. Throughout all this series of events, there is the whiff of dark dealings taking place behind closed doors in the corridors of power.

This kind of power play partly results from the otherwise positive effects of developing shared leadership teams during the previous vicar's 'reign,' just as David had done. As Mark Birchall aptly observed a decade ago:

'Shared leadership can create uncertainty about the role of the vicar. Particularly after an interregnum, lay leaders who have had to carry extra responsibilities may find it hard to let them go. Pride and jealousy, assertiveness and empire-building can prevent proper team relationships from developing'[12]

Each and every one of these facets of human nature is amply displayed in the succession narratives. What they show, however, is that where an overtly political power play has developed during the interregnum, it is vitally important to seek to discern God's candidate for the succession. This may seem obvious but in the thick of the process of Section meetings, appointing parish representatives, consultations and interviews, praying and seeking the mind of God—as Nathan did—can get neglected.

From Founding Father to Just Lawyer—Peter to James (Acts 15)

It is clear from the accounts of the early chapters of Acts that Peter was regarded as leader of the primitive church at Jerusalem (1.13-15; 2.14; 4.1-22; 5.17-42; 5.3ff). But by Acts 9 it is equally apparent that Peter's ministry had developed into that of an apostolic missionary throughout the whole Jewish area.

So, by the time of the Council of Jerusalem (15.1-21) it is James who is revealed as the Council's chairman and leader of the Jerusalem church (cf Gal 2.9, where James is named ahead of Peter and John). This view is confirmed by Paul's return visit to Jerusalem, before he is arrested, where his most important meeting is with James (21.18ff). Somewhere along the way Peter has relinquished his position as local church pastor and leader to continue with his apostolic calling.

In contemporary Anglican parlance Peter had become something like a Rector Emeritus, to James' new authoritative status as vicar. It is likely that he was counted as the twelfth apostle, despite the fact that he did not become a believer until after the Resurrection. He became known as James 'The Just' and was accorded the title of 'bishop of the bishops' by Clement.

James was a leader who could clearly be regarded as a solid (if not arch-) conservative, with a strong Jewish legal mind-set, which made him the ideal successor to Peter. Whereas Peter, 'the Rock,' was the original founding father at Jerusalem, his vocation from God was wider than this. It was Peter's great sense

---

12 Mark Birchall, 'The case for corporate leadership in the local church' in General Synod Report of a Working Party, *All Are Called—Towards a Theology of the Laity* (London: CIO Publishing, 1985) p 55.

of vision, post-Resurrection and Pentecost, that firmly established the Jerusalem church so quickly. But visionaries with apostolic callings do not make good local church leaders. By contrast, James was someone who was keen to maintain the *status quo* within a fairly rigid framework. He was, therefore, able to take the church on from its founding father, by preserving its essentially Jewish character—which was exactly what was needed there!

The lesson for a contemporary interregnum is that 'founding-father' vicars, who initiate major new visions, are not ideally followed by further visionaries. There is usually the need for a period of consolidation. The church will need a following leader who is able clearly to demarcate the boundaries of the earlier vision and keep people within them. So, if you have had a vicar with a rocklike vision, move on—you will next need to appoint someone like James, a legal expert with a praying heart, who can establish your boundaries, without getting side-lined by further radical new ideas.

Conflict Can Clear the Head—Barnabas to Paul (Acts 13.1—Acts 15.40)

At first sight the break-up of the apostolic age's 'A-Team' mission partnership looked like a tragedy. Barnabas, the great encourager, had been instrumental in getting a sceptical church hierarchy to accept that Saul of Tarsus really was a convert to Christ (Acts 9.26ff). So it was not surprising that when the Antioch church was looking to the Holy Spirit to guide them about mission, the Lord set apart the team of Barnabas and Saul for this task (Acts 13.2ff). Barnabas took Saul to his home town of Salamis in Cyprus. They crossed the island, which proved to be the cross-over point in their partnership. As a result of a major confrontation with a pagan sorcerer, Saul was given the new name of Paul.

This was his 'coming of age.' After this event it was always Paul and Barnabas (cf 13.13; 13.42). As with John the Baptist—who was the forerunner of Jesus— once the new leader fully emerged, Barnabas had to decrease as Paul increased. But there were further relationship difficulties down the road. When the pair decided to revisit all their church plants, Barnabas let his natural kindness overtake his wisdom. He wanted John Mark to accompany them, despite his proven unreliability. This led to a furious row between Paul and Barnabas over Mark. In consequence, Paul set sail with Silas while Barnabas held his ground and took Mark along. This is the last we hear of Barnabas, except in four references to him in Paul's letters. There the apostle speaks highly of him at first (1 Cor 9.6; Gal 2.1,9), but also points to a certain character flaw. Barnabas, as with so many encouragers, was easily swayed by powerful people (Gal 2.13).

Inevitably, successive vicars will have very different characters, no matter what their ability is to perform the tasks appointed to them. Paul and Barnabas were obviously both exceptionally gifted as evangelists and church planters, yet Barnabas' weakness in the face of potential conflict led to problems for others.

By contrast, Paul was definitely not someone to avoid conflict, although he also had great skills of diplomacy, when he chose to use them (Acts 17.22; 26.2). The issue is that a church that has become used to a 'Barnabas' style of leadership probably needs to address the question of how clear and firm it is in its policies and proclamation.

Of course, the 'Barnabas' character is always more likely to be adored by many of the congregation. And it is good to have vicars like Barnabas around. But, the church that appoints a series of 'sons of encouragement' is quite likely to begin soft-peddling the gospel. As with all leadership transitions there are times and seasons. Equally, it would be a very courageous church that always looked to appoint another Paul after each interregnum!

One Good Team Deserves Another—Paul/Barnabas to Judas/Silas (Acts 15.22-35)

It may seem like a footnote to the preceding narrative to focus on two minor characters from Acts like Judas and Silas. But the position that they held in the widening circle of the early church's missionary life was crucial. They epitomize one of the main features of NT ministerial leadership; it was corporate.

Judas and Silas were elders from the Jerusalem church who were dispatched to Antioch with Paul and Barnabas at the end of the Council of Jerusalem (Acts 15.22). There is some doubt as to whether Silas stayed at Antioch (v 31) but there is no doubt that they added their gifts as prophets to those of the other members of the apostolic band (v 32). This Judas only appears in the passage in Acts 15. But Silas is named as a frequent companion of Paul's in Acts and the Epistles (cf Acts 15.36ff; 16.25-39; 2 Cor 1.19), someone who shared in Paul's writing to the churches (1 Thess 1.1; 2 Thess 1.1); and probably a helper of Peter himself (1 Pet 5.12).

Clearly, teamwork was seen as essential to the early church's effective ministry. This early period of the church demonstrates that it relied on ministerial teams, which were shaped and reshaped according to the gifts that God had given.

Unfortunately, many team ministries break up as a result of changes of leadership. Such failures are partly the result of personality clashes, as between Barnabas and Saul, yet others fail because there has been insufficient attention paid—especially during interregnums—to the giftings and ministries needed to move from one good team to another.

The Child is Father to the Man—Paul to Timothy (1 and 2 Timothy)

The pastoral epistles of Paul to Timothy are models of how to nurture Christian leadership. They are also deeply moving as we see the elder statesman of the church tutoring his own 'true child in the faith' (1 Tim 1.2). These are a father's instructions to his spiritual son.

As such, one of Paul's main concerns is to encourage Timothy to accept his own position. He is not to be patronized because of his youthfulness (1 Tim 4.12). Instead, he should treat those older as parents, those younger as brothers and sisters and all classes of people according to the respect and honour they deserve (5.1-16). Paul recognizes that this young man is certainly prone to feeling weighed down by the pressures and strains of leading such a large church. So he reminds him of the spiritual foundation he has received from his mother and grandmother and through his 'ordination.' He is not to be timid, but disciplined and loving, in the power of the Holy Spirit (2 Tim 1.5ff).

Throughout these letters we are presented with the picture of a leadership transition for one of the largest and most influential new churches. But, far from Paul drafting in a heavyweight apostle from Jerusalem or Antioch, he sees that Timothy is quite able to cope, provided he stays close to the Lord.

The message is that big churches need leaders who serve a big God. Sometimes big leaders turn out to be quite unsuited to the tasks of discipling churches with a 'name.' The interregnum challenge is not to look for a 'big name' but for someone who will lead in the name of the real King.

Opening Up the Selection Box

Scripture has much to teach us about how to understand the interregnum. What I hope these biblical reflections will have done is to whet your appetite for searching the Bible to discover appropriate leadership transitions which help you to make sense of your situation. Search the Scriptures—perhaps with your outgoing incumbent—to draw parallels for your church with some of the great leaders of God's ancient people. And ask the Lord and each other, 'if that happened then, what should happen now?' In the next chapter I consider how you might do this.

4
Tools for Making Judgments

The interregnum is a period in which to make judgments, for reinstituting the time of the judges when there is no king in place. As such, I would like to introduce two programmes, of differing length, that I have developed for parish consultation work. These can be used during the interregnum, both for understanding the present and for making 'prophetic' judgments about the future.

1. Comings and Goings

Most of my parish consultancies involve me working with local churches over many months. But, I have also been called on recently to help several larger, mostly city centre, churches to begin their own processes of reflective judgment. In order to do that I have worked out a single evening reflection which can be completed in a two hour period. This is the programme, with some explanations:

Where have we come from...and where are we going?

1 *Introductions* (5 mins, including prayer and worship, as appropriate).

2 *Who am I today?* (15 mins). In this first part of the evening, participants are invited to talk in pairs about 'who they are today.' But 'today' is first specified as that day five years previously and then, as today, five years from now. For some, this brings eternity very close indeed!

The purpose of this opener is to help people to see that change always happens in the context of continuity. The radicals, who are looking for rampant change, need to see what is good from the past and the present. More conservative souls need to see that not everything is good—that was only true before the Fall!

3 *Questions for Now?* (25 mins, including feedback). In small groups, they answer some questions about where they are now:
   (1) What key words would you use to describe your church?
   (2) What are the tasks of your church?
   (3) What is the role of the clergy in fulfilling these tasks?
   (4) What is the role of the laity in fulfilling these tasks?

When they each report back they are able to see the variety of ways in which their church is currently defined.

4 *Questions for Then?* (30 mins, including feedback). After this, they answer the same questions for 'then,' five years from now.

5   *How do we move from 'Now' to 'Then'?* (20 mins). The final plenary asks about moving from now to then. Of course, this is a ridiculously brief time to engage such a large issue but the purpose of this final part of the main process is to enable a church to formally begin a process of making judgments during the interregnum.

6   *Endings* (10 mins, including prayer and worship, as appropriate).

This whole process takes just about two hours, allowing for moving around and some slippages. It needs very firm control and a keen eye on the clock. But I have found that the rigour of keeping this evening session going adds to the sense of recognizing that this is a significant moment, either during the interregnum or at some other time in the church's life. My most recent experience of running this evening was for a Midlands city centre church—not in Coventry—of a very different tradition to my own parish. They wrote back to me after the event:

'...it was fascinating to hear the unanimous claim at the end of the evening that all aspects of the church's ministry are the responsibility of both ordained and lay. "If only..." was our instinctive response. But your question "Would you have thought the same about shared ministry ten years ago?" was revealing and encouraging. Obviously attitudes have changed greatly in that period, and it takes time for practice to catch up with theory—so there is hope!'

2. Moving on from the Crossroads

One of the most important verses to me in my curacy was Jer 6.16, 'Thus says the Lord: Stand at the crossroads, and look, and ask for the ancient paths, where the good way lies; and walk in it, and find rest for your souls. But they said, "We will not walk in it"' (NAS).

This verse stimulated me to think through the challenge of how to help parishes genuinely to see the crossroads when they had reached it and to assess where the good and ancient way was, so that they could corporately walk down that way, into the paths of peace. In partial answer to that question, my lay team and I have developed a ten-stage process of parish consultations. At the heart of that process—which has been extensively used, right across our diocese—is a weekend away for a dozen key lay people from a parish.

Away with the Lay

The purpose of this time away is to help them 'stand at the crossroads and look,' so that they can report back to the clergy, PCC and parish what they have seen. It is carefully structured to enable the participants to, first, receive personal encouragement, using a tool we have devised called the 'gift card game.'[13]

We then help them to see how their giftings and personalities weave together

---

[13] Details of this and all other exercises from the weekend programme can be obtained by writing to me at The Christian Training Office, 4 Priory Row, Coventry CV1 5EX.

with the rest of that group, using an incredibly insightful tool, devised by the late James Hopewell, an American minister and anthropologist, in his classic book *Congregation*.[14] Every church group that I have used it with has been startled by the accuracy with which Hopewell's test characterizes their church. But what I have observed is that the Hopewell test also reveals what I call a 'gravitational effect' operating, whereby individuals are pulled towards the dominant spirituality of the group.

If this is correct it makes the interregnum even more significant for assessing congregational faith-world views because that is the time when one of the main 'gravitational pulls' is released and lay people often become freer in expressing their own spirituality. The question of who should follow as leader and what 'pull' they should exercise is, therefore, critical.

The Ways from the Crossroads

This leads onto the main purpose of the programme, which is to help this group of lay people assess which crossroads they are at and the paths God is calling them along. We introduce this by doing our single piece of teaching on the nature of the church.

In brief, we look at the foundational task, calling, ministry and heart that God has given to the church. From this we can see that there are essentially six foundational areas of the church's life. These six foundations of the church—worship, prayer, discipleship, fellowship, evangelism and social action—show us what the church is and the work that God requires it to do. We then seek to connect this general teaching with the specifics of this particular church, at its moment of transition, which may be the interregnum.

We do this by presenting the group with four 'models' of what any particular people of God can authentically be and do in the six areas of the church's life. These are structured to reflect:

A   a model of the church LOOKING OUTWARDS
B   a model of the church LOOKING INWARDS
C   a model of the church as a place of CHALLENGE
D   a model of the church as a place of ENCOURAGEMENT.

We give to each of these models a title and a brief description of what it would mean to be part of a church fulfilling its foundations in this distinctive way. So, for example, in the area of worship:

A   An INVITING church is OUTWARD looking
B   A EUCHARISTIC church is INWARD looking
C   A PROCLAIMING church is a place of CHALLENGE
D   A HAVEN church is a place of ENCOURAGEMENT[15]

---

14 James F Hopewell, *Congregation—Stories and Structures* (London: SCM Press, 1988).
15 Full details of all the descriptors and of this weekend consultation programme is available from the address given above.

Having introduced each of these 24 models of the church fulfilling its foundations, we carefully explain that any set of permutations can be a faithful response by the people of God to his word for them. However, no one church could be expected to walk at an even pace down all of these paths. As such, we need to ask the Lord to show us which paths are the ones for us to walk in, at what pace. It is our responsibility to make clear judgments about what sort of church we are and what sort of church the Lord is beckoning us to become.

Having outlined this systematic tool for making judgments—without their vicar-king—the rest of this key part of the programme involves the group in judging where they are—on these models—and which paths God is calling them down, over the next five years.

A summary agreement is reached about where they are and where they are being called. After this the group offers their judgments at a communion service. The final session involves doing some initial work on the training implications of how to walk from here to there, followed by making some decisions about what, when and how to report all this back to the vicar (if there is one), the PCC and parish.

I have taken some space to describe these two methods for helping congregations make judgments about future direction. Both have been used on many occasions but it is only in recent months that this has been in the context of the interregnum.

Some such systematic process for the interregnum will help to avoid the worst problems of leadership transition, when kings move. But how could this be developed in the context of an Anglican diocese or deanery? The final chapter will present a few ideas for how to institute such a process of making judgments when kings move.

5
Judging Between Kings

So far I have focused on the place of the Old Testament judges, as compared with that of the kings. In doing so it may have seemed that I have been suggesting a move away from vicars altogether. In fact I believe that would be both bad management and bad biblical theology.

First, all groups and institutions need visible leaders. They just need better ones. Second, there is no Old Testament precedent for asserting that the judges were any more personally superior than the kings. The judges were simply the mediators of divine judgment. It was the Lord God who was the only real Judge.

The key principle for handling the interregnum is to use it as a time for making judgments. It is in this context, therefore, that I want to conclude by suggesting some ways in which better judgment could be delivered to parishes during interregnums. Each of the four models introduced below recognizes that a new vicar needs to be on the way. At the same time, that should be a vicar who comes more from the collaborative end of Tannenbaum and Schmidt's spectrum, than from the ranks of monarchical dictatorships.

Using Parish Consultants

Each of the two toolkits for making judgments introduced in the previous chapter have been developed through my work as a parish consultant. Consultancy is the most familiar model for steering advice towards parishes at critical moments, such as the interregnum. It involves the conventional idea of an external consultant, who is able to offer his or her skills as a facilitator to a local church, with relatively few strings attached.

The key to unlocking this model is the perception that the external consultant is completely objective. He or she can come in, perhaps for as short a time as a single evening, to enable the parish to look with fresh eyes at who they are and where they are going. After that, the consultant leaves the parish to their own devices, and is free to bring his or her consultations to another church. They are free to implement or ignore the new insights they have received, as seems right in their own eyes.

The great advantage of this approach is that it minimizes dependency. The consultancy model should not bring a weighty pyramid of control with it. At the same time, it is helpful to have a small measure of episcopal authority and jurisdiction behind it, to give the time of judgment some *gravitas*. The main disadvantage of this approach is that it is not possible to develop alternative models of ministry within the parish. Consultancy works well for establishing objectives and delivering training programmes but it cannot really help with the essential task of facilitating new patterns of ministry.

Interim Ministers (i): Part-time Oversight

The most familiar model of helping a parish through its interregnum is that offered by the rural (or area) dean, as occasional oversight. This is, understandably, very variable. Some dioceses have an elaborately worked-out programme of training and job specification for rural deans.[16] Other dioceses leave it to the deaneries and parishes to find their own way through.

There is, however, a certain minimum oversight that a rural dean will always provide, often working alongside an archdeacon. This will involve making sure that the churchwardens feel as confident as possible about handling the interregnum. The rural dean will assist them in finding cover for services. He or she will advise about the formal and legal procedures, such as organizing Section 12 meetings, and, in case of emergency or problem, is the first line of oversight and care.

In this respect, the rural dean is there to be a sort of surrogate parent or occasional monarch. The main advantage of this is that the parish knows that there is somebody 'in authority' to help in cases of need or when specific advice is wanted. The main disadvantage of this minimal model of cover is that it cannot effectively move things on between vicars.

The fact of having the Rural Dean at hand—only a phone-call and short drive away—gives the impression that it can be more-or-less business as usual. This fig leaf of oversight, without any additional resources, inevitably means that neither the dean nor the parish officers and lay leaders are likely to want to institute any serious judgments or changes without a vicar around. Such a situation acts to perpetuate the myth of the vicar-as-king, stultifying the development process and completely missing the interregnum window of opportunity.

Interim Ministers (ii): The ECUSA Model

The veneer of interim ministry that we have through rural deans cover is not the only possible approach. Several dioceses within the Episcopal Church of the USA have pioneered schemes using fully fledged 'interim ministers.' There has even been a similar, short-lived, experiment in Manchester diocese with the same pattern of ministry.

Interim ministers are licensed by the bishop to act as a short term priest-in-charge when there is not an incumbent in post. They may be stipendiary or non-stipendiary but have a full-time bishop's special licence—under Canon law—to act as a particular parish's priest for a limited duration.

In a diocese with a fully-fledged scheme perhaps 10% of clergy posts may be filled by interim ministers. This would account for the average number of parishes that were in interregnum at any one time. Of course, the number of posts would never exactly match the proportion in interregnums, as some would always be longer than others. Nevertheless, an interim ministry scheme could be used to even out the length of vacancies.

---

16 I remember being part of a team at Anglian Regional Management Centre, devising a Rural Deans training scheme—for Norwich and Chelmsford dioceses—as long ago as 1984.

A standard licence for an interim minister should overlap both the periods of the outgoing and incoming incumbents. Thus, if a standard vacancy was put at nine months, the interim minister's special licence would probably be valid for a year. This first overlap period would allow the 'interim' to assess the leadership style and model of ministry operating as the parish moves into interregnum. The final overlap would enable the 'interim' to work with the new incumbent and lay leaders together, to hand-on the parish. This could valuably minimize the cultural discontinuities and losses that often happen at the end of interregnums.

So, what is the appropriate model of ministry for an 'interim'? Clearly they are far more than consultants or occasional overseers while being far less enduring than standard incumbents. Some of the key skills required are as much to do with understanding ethnography as they are to do with 'priestcraft.' In Bunting's terms they are a mix of his 'consultant,' 'practical theologian' and 'overseer' models. They would require the ability to develop giftings-for-ministry and help people think theologically through the implications of their crossroads experience but with the detachment of an overseer who could not afford to become the focus of too much dependency.

In many respects the best model is that proposed by Wesley Carr more than a decade ago.[17] He describes this model of ministry as a 'consultant,' for want of a better term, whose main function is to offer interpretations to those he or she is working with. I find this description quite unconvincing as a model for general parish ministry. It is far too detached and distant from the demands of mission or pastoral work. But as a model for 'interim ministry' it seems ideal.

What is, perhaps, even more remarkable is that this pattern of interim ministry is extremely close to the practice of the Old Testament judges or the workers following on from the New Testament apostles. Here were people of God sent out by the wider church to visit a particular tribe or church plant. They listened to the people and brought God's word to that faith community before moving on to the next. The model of interim ministry is entirely biblical; it accords with the best contemporary understandings of consultancy and is ideally suited to making the most of the interregnum gap.

Interim Ministerial Teams

Interim ministers might help a local church to develop away from kingship dependency during the interregnum but the major weakness of this solo ministry is that it does not offer any better model than that of traditional incumbency. Consequently, I want to suggest that the Rolls Royce ministry for an interregnum would be to institute an 'interim local ministerial team.'

Such a team would be formed from an amalgam of 'interim ministers,' other external consultants, who would usually be officers of the diocese or deanery and leaders from the local parish. This would operate as a local ministerial team. Many dioceses, such as Canterbury and Portsmouth, are experimenting with local min-

17 Wesley Carr The Priestlike Task (London: SPCK, 1985), pp 15f.

istry teams, whilst other dioceses have had such teams in place for many years, in both rural (Gloucester, Lincoln) and UPA (Liverpool) contexts.

Most other dioceses are actively looking at diversifying the range and patterns of ministry that they have, with teamwork being to the fore in almost every report. Standard arguments are that ministry teams allow for greater flexibility, develop the gifts and commitment of more people, help to give a clearer focus to informal lay ministries, model teamwork as the norm, and help to develop more appropriate leadership styles amongst parish clergy.

Given the range of perceived benefits arising from local ministerial teams it is, perhaps, surprising that more dioceses have not tackled the chief impediment to them—the fear of 'something new.' One way of gradually introducing such teams—comprehensively across a diocese—would be to start them as part of an interregnum. If the teams were introduced in the context of 'interim ministry' this would help them to be established in a short-term experimental way.

Of course, if such one-year experiments did not work then this would damage the wider credibility of ministerial teams but the period of bridging an interregnum should provide sufficient time—at a crossroads point in parish life—to more than demonstrate the worth of ministry teams. Furthermore, virtually every parish will go through an interregnum within a ten year span. So this scheme could be gradually and flexibly introduced across an entire diocese within a decade, provided the 'interims' and other potential team members were within post.

In many respects, such radical possibilities invite more questions than they answer. It has to be said that such patterns of ministry are, as yet, untried in the Church of England.

The nearest I have come to this was working as an external consultant with a team of parishioners, in a small Warwickshire village, for fifteen months. Although that work was very brief and provisional, I felt the greatest sense of achievement came when the new vicar—who is definitely not a monarchical dictator—arrived and rang me up. 'Thank the Lord,' he said, 'you got them to move on during the interregnum. That's the biggest sign of hope for me coming to this parish!'

A Season of Changes

There is no doubt that the Church of England is a rapidly changing institution. But for any organization one of the most challenging times is the point at which its leadership changes. The church is no exception, and it is this that makes the interregnum a most marvellous season for change and for establishing some of the principles and patterns of the emergent church.

We will not see God's kingdom fully come through new leadership styles, better judgments and 'interim ministerial teams.' But if at the point of our loss—which any vacancy always must be in one way or another—we can understand and acknowledge that 'the King is among us, his Spirit is here,' we will not be very far from that kingdom or from Jesus. He is the one King who never left an interregnum behind and whose crossing experience at Calvary led to the Resurrection road, from which this King has never departed.